THE PRAYING MANTIS, INSECT CANNIBAL

THE PRAYING MANTIS, INSECT CANNIBAL

Story and photographs by Lilo Hess

Charles Scribner's Sons **/** *New York*

THE PRAYING MANTIS, INSECT CANNIBAL

In autumn when the leaves have fallen and the trees and bushes are bare, we can see many things that were hidden when the foliage was lush and thick. Different types of birds' nests are in the forks of branches or on the ground where we would least suspect them to be. We can see the large globular paper homes of wasps, in which they lived and raised their young during the summer months. Furry patches on the ground are the remnants of well-concealed rabbits' nests; large bunches of dried leaves, high up in the trees, reveal the presence of squirrels. Attached to twigs and bushes we may see different kinds of cocoons and chrysalides, those marvelous constructions made by caterpillars in which they go through their strange transformation to emerge as moths or butterflies the following season.

Slender stems of tough weeds, grasses or briars may support small frothy-looking masses, some about the size of a walnut. These are the egg cases of praying mantids, large, fascinating insects that can be found in various shapes and sizes almost all over the world.

Late in the fall the female praying mantis, or mantid, selects the twigs or weeds on which she deposits her eggs. Instinctively she picks those that can withstand wind and hail and snowstorms. When she lays her eggs she usually sits head downward. With circular movements of her abdomen she whips up a bubbly, soft, creamy white froth, which she attaches securely around the twig or stem. Into its center, stacked in layers, she deposits from 40 to 400 eggs. Tiny passageways, in the form of flat plates, lead from the center through the foamy mass to the outside, where they can be seen as a seamlike ridge. The newly hatched babies must wriggle and crawl through these narrow passages to gain their freedom.

The egg mass darkens and hardens and becomes fibrous about one hour after the female has deposited her eggs. The egg-laying process usually takes from two to four hours. Sometimes a female may construct several smaller egg cases, with fewer eggs inside, several days apart. There is only one brood of mantises in one season. Each species shapes its own distinctive egg case. Some are globular, while others are more elongated; some are tiny, others about one and a half inches in diameter.

Neither snow, wind, ice, nor rain can hurt the eggs inside their marvelously insulated case. Instinctively the mantis has applied a principal of physics that man learned to understand only when a physicist named Benjamin Thompson, Count Rumford, who lived from 1753 to 1814, made a curious experiment. He whipped egg white to a stiff meringue and inserted in its center a piece of frozen cheese. He baked this in an oven until it was hot and brown. Then he cut his "baked Alaska" open and found that the cheese was still frozen. The tiny air bubbles in the beaten egg white acted as insulation and kept the cheese cold. The frothy mass that the praying mantis whips up does the same job of insulation but in reverse; it keeps the eggs from freezing.

Not all egg cases survive the winter. Squirrels, mice, opossums, foxes, skunks, and raccoons and some birds will eat them, and the eggs inside, when their regular food supplies are scarce.

Early one morning in June, when the air is warm, the baby mantises are ready to emerge. They wriggle and push through the wafer-like rows of plates in a steady stream, resembling molasses being poured from a jug. They emerge headfirst, their

legs folded tightly against their bodies; and each is encased in a thin sheath. From a gland in their abdomen flows a pair of short, fine silken threads which stay attached at one end to the egg case. A baby mantis will hang suspended from these threads as if exhausted for just a second or two before it bursts open its cocoonlike sheath and frees its limbs.

Forming a living chain the mantises dangle and swing in the breeze and struggle to reach the nearest branch or leaf. So great is their haste to get away from the egg-case nursery that they run, jump, tumble, or fall over their sisters and brothers that are still emerging. There is good reason for their haste, the slow ones might be devoured immediately by the stronger, more advanced individuals.

The newly hatched babies, usually called nymphs, are only slightly larger than mosquitos. Their bodies are soft and cream-colored, and they have big dark eyes. They look like fairy ghosts in the pale light of the morning. The nymphs are tiny replicas of their parents, but have no wings.

If the egg mass of the Chinese mantis, for instance, contains hundreds of eggs, the hatching process may take several hours. Other species may take several days. When all the babies have emerged and dispersed, only the silken threads and the cast-off transparent skins remain dangling from the egg case.

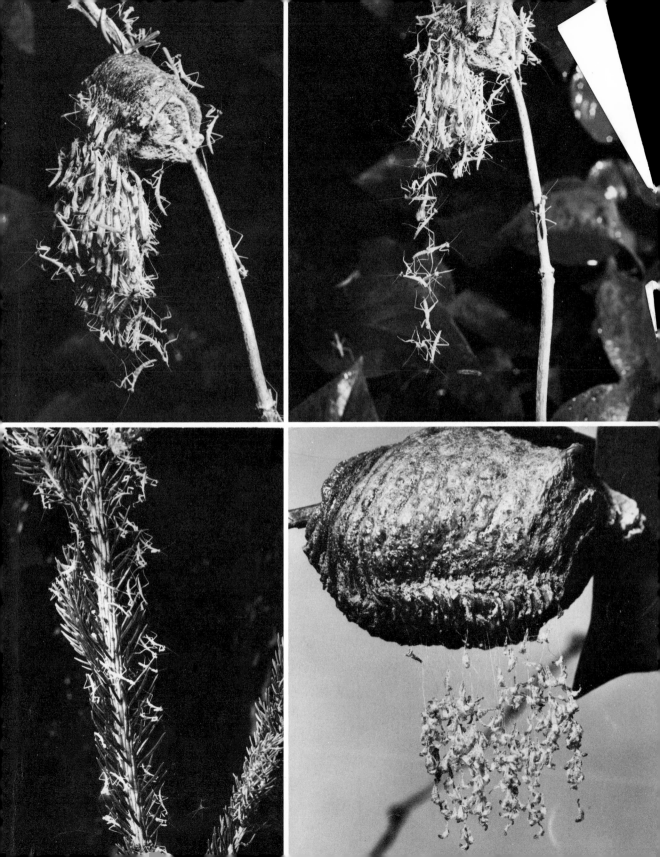

Although a large, fully grown mantis has very few enemies, the baby mantids are very vulnerable during hatching and for several days afterward. Some species of ants run up the stalks and devour the babies while they are still unable to defend themselves. Birds, some small mammals, frogs, toads, and lizards as well as some insects and spiders also feast on the tiny mantises. A heavy rainstorm can crush and kill the fragile nymphs. Since so many mantids hatch every year, the world

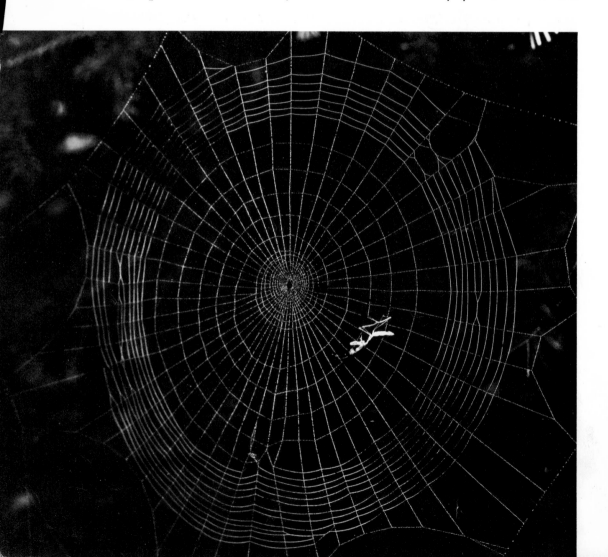

would be overrun with these insects if nature did not have its own way of retaining the balance. The babies that survive the first week of their lives have a good chance of reaching maturity.

A half hour after hatching, the soft bodies of the nymphs harden and their colors darken to brown or green. They blend in so perfectly with the foliage and branches that they are extremely hard to see.

In the Orient, people think that the mantises grow on trees in the form of leaves, and that they become insects only when they break loose from the branches at maturity. This curious belief probably comes from the fact that the mantids are very well camouflaged and become noticeable only when they are fully grown.

The baby mantids start their search for food a day after hatching, and they prove themselves as aggressive and gluttonous as their reputation claims. Juicy aphids, leafhoppers, tiny flies, and mosquitos are their first prey. They seldom run after their victims, but rather sit quietly until the "food" is within their reach. After a few weeks they consume small caterpillars, regular house flies, and small beetles.

Mantises, like other insects, wear their skeletons on the outside. As they grow, their skins become too tight and are cast off—about every two weeks. Each time they emerge larger and stronger.

Early in the fall the large mantis is ready to shed its skin for the last time. This is the most critical molt in its life. If the atmosphere has been too dry or if the insect did not have enough water to drink during the previous weeks, its skin might not come off easily, or its newly formed wings might be stunted. If all goes well, the mantis securely suspends itself head-down, from a branch or weed. It presses its head forward and upward until its mouth reaches its underside, where the thorax joins the head. The mantis chews an opening into the loose skin, which simultaneously splits on top of its thorax and along its back. The mantis frees its head and long antennae first, then as the insect pushes its body forward in pulses, the old skin slides back and the legs are pulled out from the casing. Unlike the body covering, the leg casings do not split open.

The newly emerged large mantis clings to its cast-off skin while its new one hardens. The wings are wrinkled little stubbles. After about thirty minutes the insect crawls away from the old skin, once more attaching itself securely to a twig or similar support. This time however it is usually head upward.

It now starts the slow process of unfolding and stretching its wings. It might take an hour until the soft, pale wings are smooth, hanging loosely like a veil. After another hour, these too harden, darken, and are folded in the normal position. A

18

large mantis is a powerful flier, and some have a wingspread of six or seven inches. Most of our American mantises have wings, but a few species are wingless all their lives.

The praying mantis is related to the grasshopper, cockroach, katydid, and stick insect. There are about seventeen different kinds of mantises native to the United States. In 1896 the first foreign mantids were seen in the U.S.A. Other species were noticed in 1899 and 1926. One species had come from Europe, and two others from the Orient. They probably had arrived in this country as stowaways. No one knows for sure. The egg cases might have been attached to imported plants or weeds used as hay or packing. When the baby mantises hatched, they found the climate favorable and the food supply ample. Now these three species are found in almost every part of the United States. They are our largest species, about three to five inches long.

There are about 1,800 species of praying mantises distributed all over the world. Most of them live in temperate or tropical regions, but explorers have found some of them as high as 16,000 feet above sea level. Their appearance and size vary almost as much as their numbers. Some are less than an inch long, while others—mostly tropical—may be over ten inches long. Almost all praying mantids are well camouflaged, resembling or blending with leaves, twigs, or even blades of grass among which they lie in wait to ambush their insect victims. The majority of mantids are brown or green.

The rare pink mantis from Malaysia resembles in its color and shape the orchids among which it lives.

Some tropical species have a flattened part on their bodies, which makes them resemble leaves; other species look like pieces of lichen or flakes of bark. Some mimic the harmless, plant-eating stick insect; others have large eye-spots on their wings to fool their predators.

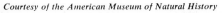

Mantises have been well known since ancient times. Their curious looks and odd behavior have aroused people's imaginations, and many supernatural powers, evils as well as virtues, have been attributed to them.

In Africa it was believed that the mantis could bring the dead back to life, and therefore it was worshipped by many. Others believed that if a mantis settled on a person, this person was favored by the heavens and should be considered a saint.

Mouffet, a seventeenth-century naturalist, said that French country people believed that if a lost child should ask its way of this insect, the mantis would stretch out its long legs to indicate the right direction and never make a mistake.

Mantis is a Greek word meaning "prophet," "diviner," or "clairvoyant." People of the middle ages believed that the insect spent most of its time in prayer and that it was a great worshipper of God. Turks and Arabs insisted that the praying mantis always prays with its face turned toward Mecca.

The praying mantis with its pious-looking pose, its quiet manner, and camouflaged shape is really a wolf in sheep's clothing. Although it is harmless to man and beasts, to other insects it is a formidable enemy. The mantis is not only deadly to insects smaller than itself, but it will tackle large ones as well. It is extremely courageous and will attempt to strike even at small mammals, but naturally does not hurt them.

In the fall of the year the mantis can be found almost anywhere; it might cling to window screens, sit on porches or mailboxes. It might be spotted on street signs in a city or on the thirtieth floor of a skyscraper. In the country it can be found in places that have a good food supply—in meadows where there are many crickets and grasshoppers, or in a barn or stable where flies congregate. It might even be bold enough to perch on a horse's mane or tail, waiting for flies to approach. Sometimes mantises visit hornets' nests or apiaries, waiting patiently near a hive or in nearby flowers for a honeybee to come within reach. When a mantis catches a bee, it holds it so tightly that the bee is usually unable to use its sting. But once in a while a wasp, hornet, or bee does sting the mantis, who then quickly drops its prey and licks its wound.

The mantis has a small triangular head with large eyes. It is the only insect that can turn its head freely from right to left or up and down. It can also look over its shoulder. When a mantis turns its head to follow the movement of a person or to look straight into the eyes of an observer, it seems to have an inquisitive, personable expression.

Scientists have worked long to determine how a mantis can judge with such remarkable, never-failing accuracy the size, the distance, and the direction of movement of its prey. They have now found that this is achieved by the position of its head and the binocular vision of its eyes. When a mantis spots an insect it wants to catch, it must turn its head so that its eyes, which themselves are immovable, look directly at the victim. This motion disturbs and bends small hairs at the side of its head and a message is sent from the bent hairs to the central nervous system, which in turn sends a message to the forelegs, directing them how far to reach and what size the victim is. A mantis with only one eye or vision in only one eye probably could not catch its food properly. It might overshoot small prey, and undershoot large prey, since it would judge distance only by the size.

The eyes of the mantis are compound eyes. Each one is composed of hundreds of tiny facets. Each facet produces a small part of the entire picture. Altogether they produce a mosaic view. The picture is probably blurred except for one central point because insect eyes cannot change focus like the eyes of man. Since the mantis can turn its head, it probably can scan about 300 degrees.

In addition to the compound eyes the mantis has three little dots arranged in a triangle on the front of its head. These are simple eyes which have only one facet. Their function is not really known but it is believed that they supplement the compound eyes in response to light.

The eyes of the mantis are usually light green or tan, but at dusk a remarkable change occurs. The pigment in the eye becomes dark and looks deep brown or almost black. Eyes of nocturnal animals change at night to permit the ultra-sensitive nerve cells in the eye to make full use of all available light, including that of the moon and the stars.

The praying mantis often hunts at night and can be seen near lighted lamps on porches or near streetlights, catching night-flying insects which are attracted to the light.

The mantis has no ear in the sense we know of ears. Its sensitive antennae, or feelers, help it to hear and probably also to smell.

Like all insects the praying mantis has six legs, but its front legs are very different from its other legs. They are large and greatly modified. They consist of five segments, two of which are armed with sharp toothlike spines that can grasp and hold a victim as though in a vise. The front legs can be stretched out and held rigid or can be folded so that the segments are side by side and raised. This latter position is the one which gives the appearance of hands held in prayer and for which the mantis has become so well known.

When the mantis is ready to strike at a victim, the front legs dart out with lightning speed and the spikes and strong muscles hold even the most vigorously struggling prey.

33

The mantis is not very particular what kind of insect it eats; even the monarch butterfly, the stinkbug, and other badtasting insects are eaten by this insect glutton.

The victim is devoured alive, the mantis holding it like a person would hold an ear of corn, with either one or both forelegs. After a meal the mantis usually washes itself like a kitten, cleaning each leg carefully with its mandibles and finally pulling its antennae down with its foreleg, cleaning them as well.

The mandibles are a pair of jawlike appendages, placed at the side of the mouth. They are horny and form the grinding surface. The lower part of the mouth is shaped so that it can manipulate and direct the food toward the mouth.

The praying mantis is not only a greedy consumer of various insects but is also cannibalistic, which means it will eat its own kind if it gets the chance. Larger individuals eat the smaller ones; the stronger mantis will eat the weaker ones. This habit has endeared them to the Asmat people, a native tribe that lives in a small area on the southern coast of New Guinea. The Asmats were fierce headhunters and cannibals until after World War II. All their neighbors were afraid of them. The Asmats painted, modeled, or carved different animals as symbols of honored ancestors or of man in general. The praying mantis was a favorite since it was fearless and cannibalistic just as the

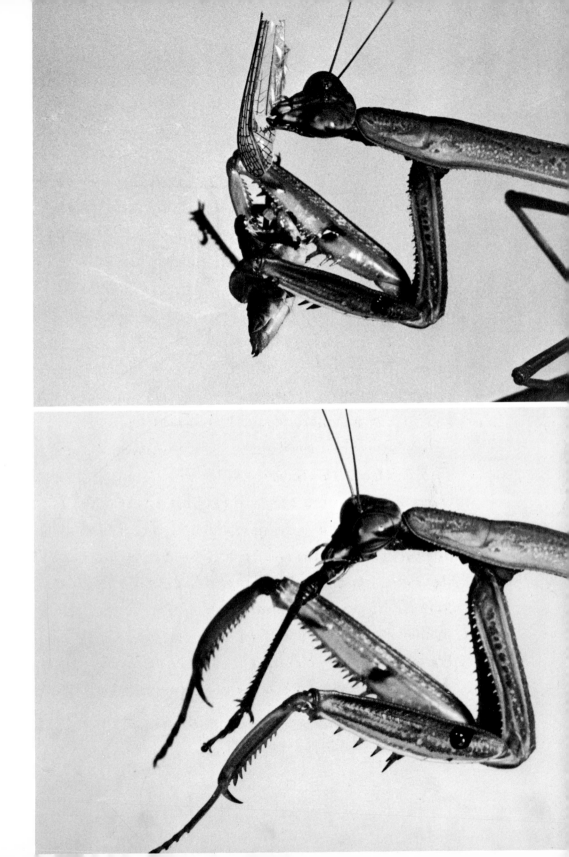

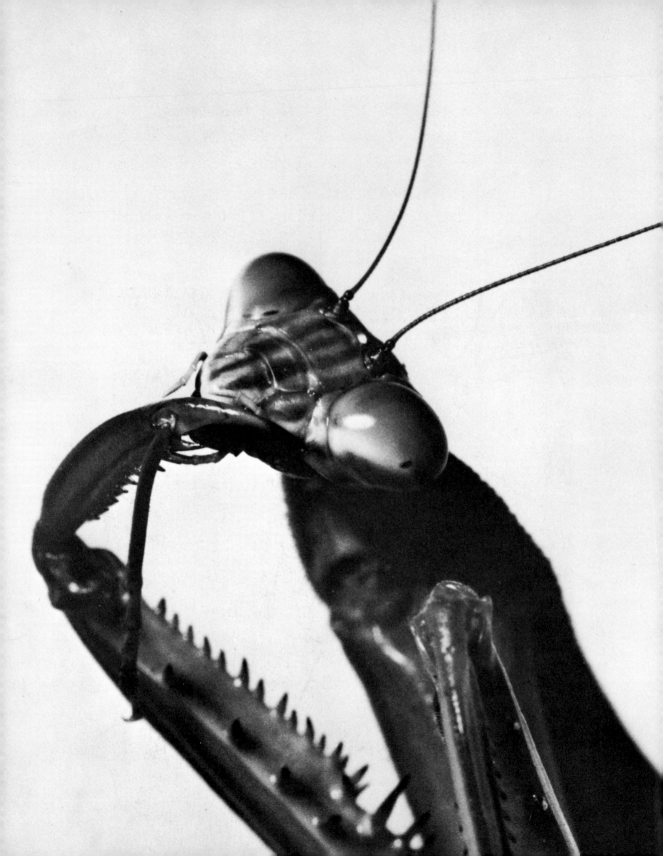

Asmats themselves. The mantis figure was used to decorate shields, drums, spears, and prows of canoes. Even their drinking vessels often had a carving of a mantis as a handle. They usually portrayed the mantis with an almost human head. The picture shows the carved and painted figure of a mantis on the prow of a canoe.

In the fall, the mantis is ready to seek a mate. At this time the sexes are easily distinguishable. The female's abdomen has become so large with eggs that she has to select stronger weeds and branches on which to perch, to support her weight. The male remains very slim. When he approaches her, he has to be careful not to get within reach of her dangerous forelegs. The female does not seem to recognize the male as a suitor and would grab and eat him if she could reach him. The male has to approach unobserved from the rear in order to mate successfully. He clasps the female around her body with his forelegs and then lifts each of his hindlegs cautiously onto her back. Sometimes the mating pair will hang upside down. The male transfers to the female a capsule that contains the spermatozoa which later fertilize her eggs. The male and female usually cling together for several hours. After mating, the male must be just as cautious in leaving his bride as he was when he approached her. First he disengages his forelegs and hangs or stands on his hindlegs. Then suddenly he releases all four hindlegs at once, falls or flutters to the ground, and runs or flies away as quickly as possible. Not all males are lucky enough to escape. Some are decapitated and consumed by the female right after or even during the act of mating.

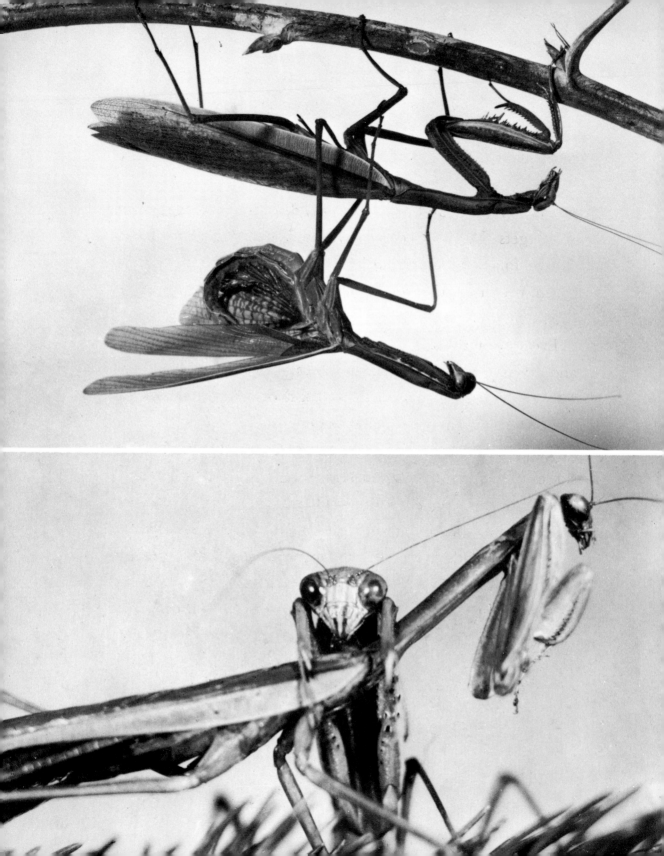

Several days after mating, the female lays her eggs and then walks away and has nothing more to do with her future offspring.

The praying mantis lives for only one season. When the weather gets cold and its food supply dwindles, this super-sized insect gets sluggish and drowsy and loses its appetite. It sits quietly for many hours and its movements are extremely slow. Then, usually during a frosty night in November, the mantis dies.

Even if a mantis is brought indoors in the fall, kept warm and given plenty of live insects to eat, it will live only a few weeks more than it would have out of doors. Nature's clock has run down and cannot be turned back.

The praying mantis is one of the few insects that can be kept successfully as a pet. Although it is doubtful that it learns to recognize its keeper, it will get tame and become accustomed to being handled. The mantis can be allowed the freedom of the house provided no other pets are near. Dogs and cats might playfully chase it or step on it. The mantis likes to perch in odd places: on curtains, chairs, sofas, or table lamps, on cookpots, and even on the bathtub. Houseplants in a window make a favorite resting place and at Christmastime a long-lived pet mantis might perch for hours among the ornaments of a Christmas tree.

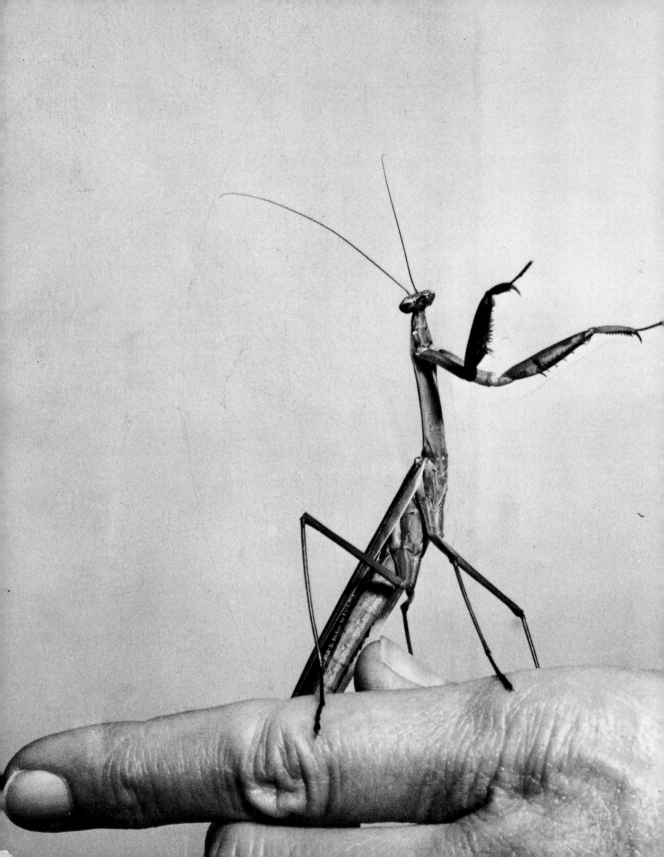

It is best to keep a mantis in a cage unless someone is around to keep an eye on it. A fish tank with a wire mesh top or covered with cheesecloth, a terrarium, or a wire mesh cage makes a fine home. Since the insect is so large, the cage must be big enough to allow room to move about comfortably. A mason jar or similar container should never be used for any length of time.

The home of the mantis must contain branches or twigs for it to climb on, but not so many that it has to contort its body for it might break its wings when it moves about. Leaves are not necessary for its well-being, but can be used for decoration. Plastic flowers or greens will serve as well. Sand or soil should not be put into the bottom of the cage, since most insects that are used as food for the mantis will burrow into it and cannot be caught.

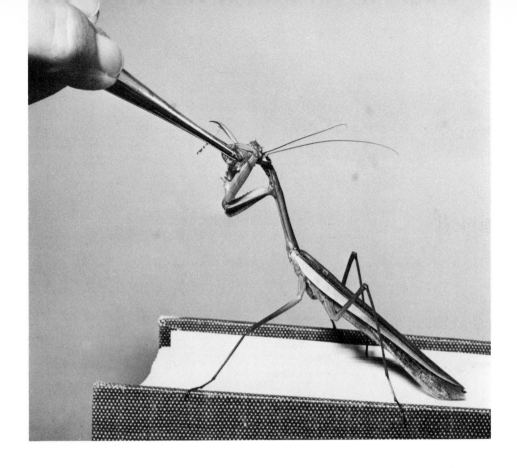

Feeding this tigress of the insect world presents the biggest problem. The mantis is always ready to eat and catching enough live food to satisfy it is almost a full-time job. If the food offered is not quite to its taste, it will drop it after just a few nibbles. In the summer and early fall, grasshoppers, flies, crickets, moths, katydids, and small beetles are easily obtained if one lives in the country or suburbs. City dwellers will have to buy crickets from local pet stores, cricket ranches, or fish-bait stores. Mealworms, which are usually available at pet stores, are not always relished by the mantis but it will eventually eat them if no other food is available. Small pieces of lean hamburger held with forceps and made to "wriggle" can also be fed.

Mantids drink a lot of water, and pet insects more often die from dehydration than from lack of food. Water sprinkled on the sides of a glass cage or on twigs and foliage is one way of "watering" the mantis. They can also be trained to drink from an eyedropper or spoon. As soon as it realizes that water is there, the mantis will bend its head down low and drink long and slowly. The mantis does not seem to learn to drink out of a dish of water left in the cage.

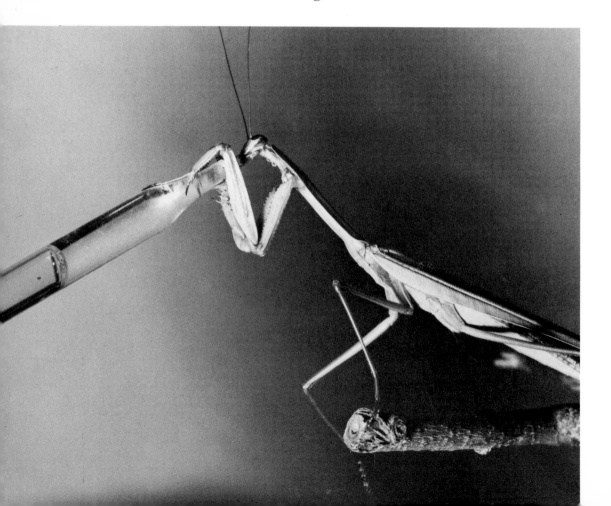

Raising praying mantises from eggs is a good project for the classroom, or it can be done at home. Egg cases can be kept in the refrigerator until one has enough small insects to feed the newly hatched babies. Fruitfly cultures should be started before the mantises hatch. It is best, however, to wait until spring with this project since several hundred newly hatched mantises can scarcely be fed. Only a few should be kept for study, the others liberated outdoors. The babies hatch about four to five weeks after the egg mass has been removed from the refrigerator. Egg masses can be bought from biological supply houses or plant nurseries.

It has recently become popular to buy praying mantis egg cases for farms and gardens to control insect pests in a natural way, eliminating the use of harmful sprays. Unfortunately the mantis destroys beneficial insects as well.

Wherever the praying mantis with its sanctimonious looks and cutthroat ways appears, people will react with admiration, fear, curiosity, or superstition. Even today, the mantis is still called *Lou Prègo-Dieu* (the animal that prays to God), Mule-killer (the insect that poisons livestock), Devil's Rear Horse, and Soothsayer. But no one who has ever been acquainted with this personable insect has failed to be intrigued by it.